November

Happy Birthday
EMILY!

Love,
Cliff
& Beth

Written by Ruthie May
Illustrated by Leigh HOBBS

Stew a Cockatoo

My Aussie Cookbook

LITTLE HARE
www.littleharebooks.com

We Australians love our slang. 'Arvo tea' sounds friendlier than 'afternoon tea' and 'fair dinkum' is more fun to say than 'genuine'. This book is jam-packed with Aussie slang. If you come across something you haven't heard before, don't worry, now is your chance to pick up some you-beaut lingo you can use with your mates.

For Norm Corker – the best sav stew maker in all of Oz. On ya, Gramps! —RM

Little Hare Books
an imprint of
Hardie Grant Egmont
85 High Street
Prahran, Victoria 3181, Australia

www.littleharebooks.com

Copyright © text Little Hare Books 2010
Copyright © illustrations Leigh Hobbs 2010
Text by Ruthie May
Additional design elements by Luke Kelly

First published 2010

All rights reserved. No part of this publication may be reproduced, stored in a retrieval system or transmitted in any form or by any means, electronic, mechanical, photocopying, recording or otherwise, without the prior written permission of the publisher.

National Library of Australia Cataloguing-in-Publication entry
May, Ruthie.
Stew a cockatoo : my Aussie cookbook / written by Ruthie May; illustrated by Leigh Hobbs.
9781921541513 (hbk.)
For primary school age.
Cookery – Juvenile literature.
Cookery – Australia.
Hobbs, Leigh.
641.5994

Designed by Vida & Luke Kelly
Produced by Pica Digital, Singapore
Printed through Phoenix Offset
Printed in Shen Zhen, Guangdong Province, China, August 2010

5 4 3 2 1

Table of Contents

- 4   Cooee, G'Day, Howya Goin'?
- 5   Useful Cook's Tools
- 6   'Ave a Drink, Ya Mug!
- 8   The Bread Spread
- 10   Morning Tea for Lords and Bush Pigs
- 12   Bikkies for the Boys
- 14   Arvo Tea at Auntie Beryl's
- 16   From the Esky
- 18   Horse Doovers
- 20   Whacko the Chook!
- 22   The Great Aussie Icon: Dinky-di Meat Pie
- 24   Grandpa Bruce's Great Aussie BBQ
- 26   It's a Rissole, Love!
- 28   Bangers, Snags and Mystery Bags
- 30   Fish 'n' Chips Down Under
- 32   Bush Tucker
- 34   From Over Yonder to Down Under
- 36   Dessert Dames
- 38   All Over, Pavlova
- 40   Index

Cooee, g'day, howya goin'?

Cooee, G'Day, Howya Goin'?

This is a book for the whole family—kids and oldies alike. It's full of old-time Aussie recipes, with a few new ones added in. Some you will have heard of, like Damper (page 9) and Lamingtons (page 11). Others are brand-spanking-new versions of golden oldies, like Edna Split (page 37) and Roo Doo in a Patty Case (page 15). Some of the recipes have come all the way Down Under from faraway places like Italy and Mexico, but here they are given a you-beaut Aussie twist. All the recipes celebrate the grub that Aussies love to eat—from barbies with the rellies to fine dining with mates beside the pool.

There are just three important things to remember when cooking from this book:

1 If you're a kid, you'll need an oldie (a grown-up) to help—a grandad, gran, mum, dad, brother, sis, auntie, unc or cuz. Cooking can be dangerous—there are hot stoves, hot oil, camp fires, knives and blenders. You'll also need some help getting the jumbuck in the tuckerbag. So make sure you always have someone to help.

2 If you're an oldie, you'll need a kid to help. Cooking can be hard work— there are pots to scrub, spuds to peel and things to chop. You just don't know when an anklebiter might come in handy. And besides, they will make the kitchen much more fun.

3 Cooking tucker is easy, just 'avago!

'Ave a Drink, Ya Mug!

Living in Australia is thirsty work, especially during the hot summers! You'll want a few cool drinks up your sleeve. Try these bonza drinks. And don't forget billy tea, it's more refreshing than you might think on a hot summer's day!

Grab a friend and a billy, and bat the breeze. It's paradise.

Billy tea is different to all other teas. The traditional smoky flavour comes from the tin sitting on the coals; the smoke curls into the tin and flavours the tea.

Billy Tea

Serves 2

You will need a billy can, a sturdy forked stick and a camp fire

Ingredients

2 cups water
3 teaspoons black tea
Sugar and milk, if you like

Method

Fill the billy can with the water. Wait for the fire to burn down to red-hot coals and, using the forked stick, place the billy on the coals. Wait for the water to boil, then remove billy from coals using the forked stick. Add the tea (a teaspoon for each person and one for the pot) and allow to brew for about 3 minutes. Pour into 2 mugs. Add a teaspoon of sugar and a splash of milk, if that's how you like it.

Berry Shake

Serves 2-4

You will need a blender

Ingredients

1/2 cup frozen berries
2 cups milk
2 tablespoons honey
2 scoops vanilla ice-cream
1/4 teaspoon vanilla essence
4 ice cubes
Crushed nuts (optional)

Method

Throw everything in the blender. Blend. Drink.

Redback Spider

Serves 1

Ingredients

2 scoops vanilla ice-cream
600 ml red creaming soda

Method

Place the ice-cream in a tall milkshake glass (or the biggest glass you can find in the cupboard). Fill slowly with the creaming soda. It's best to drink your Redback Spider with a straw—it's so bubbly, creamy and spidery you don't want to drink too much at once!

The Bread Spread

Damper was invented by the Indigenous Australians. They used to make their bush bread from wild grains and nuts. When white people came, drovers and stockmen used flour to make bread the way the Indigenous Australians did, cooking it in the coals of an open camp fire. White folks called it damper.

People still cook damper over open fires in the bush. But mostly, Aussies cook this old bush tucker in their modern kitchen ovens. We're going to show you how to bake it that way. One day, you should ask an oldie—preferably an Indigenous Australian oldie—to show you how it is cooked in a fire.

Damper with Cocky's Joy

Serves 4

You will need a mixing bowl, measuring cups and spoons, a flour sifter and a large baking tray. And very clean hands!

Ingredients

3 cups self-raising flour
1 teaspoon salt
2 teaspoons sugar
1 tablespoon chilled butter
1 cup water (or milk)
Cocky's Joy (golden syrup)
Butter, extra

Method

Preheat the oven to 200°C and grease a large baking tray.

Sift the flour and salt into a mixing bowl. Mix in the sugar.

Using your fingers, rub the butter into the flour mixture. Add the water (or milk), a little at a time, mixing all the time with your hands (but don't lick your fingers!). You want the dough to be a bit gooey, but not runny.

Place the dough on a floured bench and shape it into a flat ball. Place on the baking tray and bake for 30 minutes or until golden brown on top.

Eat your damper while it is still warm. It tastes best with butter and drizzled with Cocky's Joy.

Aussie Chrissie Damper

Follow the directions for Damper with Cocky's Joy, but before you cook your dough, shape it into a star. Poke in some sultanas. This will make a beaut spotty-star Christmas damper.

Auntie's Chrissie-themed damper.

Billy Loaf

Preheat the oven to 180°C. Grease and flour a 2-litre billy can (ask an oldie to show you how).

Make one batch of Damper with Cocky's Joy, but instead of shaping it into a ball, place it in the billy and put the lid on. Bake in the oven for 45 minutes. Ask an oldie to check on it after 30 minutes by removing from the oven and peeking under the lid. If it hasn't gone golden, place back in the oven for a further 15 minutes.

If you want your Billy Loaf to be even tastier, add 1 cup of mixed dried fruit to the dough mix before you put it in your billy can.

Morning Tea for Lords and Bush Pigs

In Australia, there's always time for a cuppa and a bit of chitchat.

Lord Lamington was the governor of Queensland in the early days. He was also a clumsy old codger. One day at morning tea, he accidentally dropped his cake into a pot of runny chocolate. He ate it and thought it tasted better dipped in chocolate than it did plain. The only problem was, it made his fingers messy. He suggested that his cook dip pieces of cake in chocolate and then roll them in desiccated coconut so they wouldn't be so sticky. That's how some folk think the lamington was invented.

Bush-Pig Fairy Bread

Makes about 24 pieces

You will need cookie-cutter shapes

Ingredients
12 slices white bread
100 g butter, softened
Hundreds and thousands

Method
Spread the bread slices evenly with the butter. Use different-shaped cutters (preferably a pig shape) to cut shapes from the bread. Place the hundreds and thousands on a plate. Press the bread, butter-side down, into the hundreds and thousands to coat. Eat with all your bush-pig friends.

Lord Lamington's Lamingtons

Makes 16 large lamingtons

You will need a mixing bowl and a cooling rack

I say, what an absolute delight!

Ingredients

500 g icing sugar
1/3 cup cocoa
15 g butter
1/2 cup milk
3 cups desiccated coconut
2 ready-made square sponge cakes

Method

Sift the icing sugar and cocoa into a heatproof bowl. Add the butter and milk. Stir over a pan of hot water until the icing is smooth and glossy.

Spread the coconut on a large plate. Trim the brown crust from the top and sides of the cake. Cut each cake into eight evenly sized square pieces. Stick a fork into one piece of cake and dip it into the warm icing. Allow any excess icing to drip off. Toss the iced cake in the coconut, to coat. Place on a cooling rack to set. Repeat with the remaining pieces of cake.

Pikelets

Makes about 24 pikelets

You will need 2 mixing bowls, a frying pan and an eggflip

Ingredients

1 cup self-raising flour
1/4 teaspoon bicarbonate of soda
3 tablespoons white sugar
1 egg
3/4 cup milk
2 teaspoons butter, melted
Butter, extra
Your favourite jam

Method

Sift the flour and bicarbonate of soda into a mixing bowl and stir in the sugar. In a separate bowl, beat the egg with the milk and melted butter. Slowly mix the wet mixture into the dry mixture until the batter is smooth.

Grease a frying pan with a little bit of butter. Drop a tablespoon of batter into the pan, and cook until golden brown on the bottom, with bubbles appearing on top. Turn with an eggflip and cook the other side for a minute or so. Cook in batches of three or four. Spread with butter and jam to serve.

Bikkies for the Boys

Australia loves its Anzacs and its Anzac bikkies.

The Anzac biscuit was first made during World War I, when more than 330 000 Australians served in the armed forces. Along with the New Zealanders, Australian soldiers were half a world away from their home, and any packages of food sent to them from their families arrived mouldy and inedible. So the women back home in Australia—the mums, grannies, sisters, wives and girlfriends of the soldiers—came up with the Anzac biscuit. It was hard and full of sugar and it lasted the long journey by sea to the trenches in France, Gallipoli and even Egypt.

Anzac Day, April 25, is the day when we remember the hard work, bravery and sacrifice of the Australian soldiers, doctors and nurses who have served in conflicts throughout our history. Making Anzac bikkies and sharing them with your friends is a good way to celebrate the day.

Anzac Biscuits

Makes about 24 biscuits

You will need a baking tray, 2 mixing bowls and a cooling rack

Ingredients

1 cup raw sugar

1 cup rolled oats

1 cup desiccated coconut

1 cup plain flour

125 g butter, melted

1 teaspoon bicarbonate of soda

1 tablespoon Cocky's Joy (golden syrup)

2 tablespoons boiling water

Method

Preheat the oven to 150°C and grease a baking tray.

Mix the sugar, oats, coconut and flour in a bowl. Pour in the melted butter and mix thoroughly. In a separate bowl, combine the bicarbonate of soda, Cocky's Joy and boiling water, and add to the oat mixture. Mix well.

Drop tablespoonfuls of mixture onto the baking tray, leaving a gap between each one, and bake for 20 minutes. Allow to cool on a cooling rack.

Grandpa Bruce's personal assistant does the Anzac biscuit taste-test.

Arvo Tea at Auntie Beryl's

Pass us the jam, love!

Did you know that there are scone-baking competitions all around Australia? Many are held in country towns. Why not practise some of the recipes here and try your luck? You could even organise a competition amongst your neighbours and friends!

Beryl's Bonza Scones

Makes about 30 scones

You will need 2 baking trays, a rolling pin, a 4 cm round cookie cutter, a pastry brush and very clean hands

Ingredients

3 cups self-raising flour
1 teaspoon salt
60 g chilled butter, cubed
1 cup milk
Milk, extra
Your favourite jam
Whipped cream

Method

Preheat the oven to 220°C and grease 2 baking trays. Sift the flour and salt into a bowl. Rub the butter into the flour until you have a crumbly mixture. Make a well in the centre and mix in the milk to make a soft dough. Turn the dough out onto a floured surface. Knead lightly and quickly, until soft, then roll out to a thickness of 2 cm. Cut into rounds with the cutter. Place the rounds on the baking trays. Brush the tops lightly with milk. Bake for 10–15 minutes, until risen and golden. Allow to cool on the trays, but while they are still warm serve with jam and cream.

Queensland Blue Pumpkin Scones

Makes about 20 scones

You will need 2 baking trays, a rolling pin, a 4 cm round cookie cutter and a pastry brush

Proud Beryl with another scone triumph.

Ingredients

1 1/2 tablespoons butter, softened
1/2 cup sugar
1 egg
1 cup cooked and mashed pumpkin (preferably Queensland Blue)
2 cups self-raising flour, sifted
Milk
Your favourite jam
Whipped cream

Method

Preheat the oven to 220°C and grease 2 baking trays. Using an electric beater, cream the butter and sugar. Add the egg and mix until light and fluffy. Mix in the pumpkin. Add the flour and mix well. Turn mixture out onto a floured surface. Roll out to a thickness of 2 cm. Cut into rounds with the cutter. Place the rounds on the baking trays. Brush the tops lightly with milk. Bake for 15–20 minutes, until risen and golden. Allow to cool on the trays, but while they are still warm serve with jam and cream.

Roo Doo in a Patty Case (chocolate crackles)

Makes about 20

You will need a large mixing bowl, a saucepan, 20 paper patty cases and a baking tray

Ingredients

125 g copha
2 cups rice bubbles
3/4 cup sifted icing sugar
1 1/2 tablespoons sifted cocoa
1/2 cup desiccated coconut

Method

Melt the copha in a saucepan over low heat. Allow to cool. Mix the remaining ingredients in a large bowl. Stir in the copha and mix well. Spoon the mixture into paper patty cases. Place the filled cases on a tray and refrigerate until set.

From the Esky

In the late 1800s, people loved eating jellies. But they didn't have refrigerators to set the jellies in. Instead, they would lower the jelly, in its jelly mould, down a well where it was chilly and dank. The trouble was that frogs also liked the cool, dark depths of wells. Frogs would sometimes jump into the jellies—and get stuck there!

Without an esky on a summer's day, your drinks are warm and your icy pole is a puddle.

Frogs in the Billabong

Serves 6

Ingredients
1 packet green or blue jelly
6 chocolate or lolly frogs

Method
Make green or blue jelly according to the packet instructions. Allow the mixture to cool but not set. Stick frogs into the jelly. Leave to set in the fridge.

Joe Blakes in the Billabong

Follow Frogs in the Billabong recipe, but use snake lollies instead of frogs.

Joe Blake is rhyming slang for snake.

Billabong Surprise

Follow Frogs in the Billabong recipe, but put a combination of snake, frog and dinosaur lollies into the jelly mixture.

Dinky-di Icy Poles

Makes about 12 icy poles

You will need 2 icy-pole trays and a blender

Ingredients

2 kiwifruits, peeled
2 oranges, peeled and seeds removed
2 apples, cored
1 punnet strawberries, hulled
2 passionfruits
1/2 cup pineapple juice or orange juice

Method

Chop the kiwifruit, oranges and apples into chunks. Place in blender, along with the strawberries, passionfruit pulp, pineapple juice or orange juice. Blend. Pour evenly into the icy-pole trays and put on the lids with sticks. Freeze overnight before serving.

Banana Benders

Makes 8

You will need 8 wooden skewers, cling wrap and a tray

Ingredients

8 ripe bananas, peeled
500 g chocolate (white, dark or milk), broken into pieces
Crushed nuts (optional)

Method

Line a tray with cling wrap. Push a wooden skewer up the length of each banana. Arrange bananas on the tray and freeze overnight.

Melt the chocolate in a heatproof bowl over a pan of simmering water, stirring all the time. Remove the bananas from the freezer and coat each banana in the melted chocolate. Dip in crushed nuts, if using, and place back on the tray. Freeze for a further 30 minutes before serving.

Horse Doovers

Something people eat, not something horses do.

Horse Doovers is a silly Aussie way of saying *hors d'oeuvres*, which is the fancy French way of saying 'nibbles'. *Hors d'oeuvres* are the little snacks that you might eat before dinner. At most Aussie barbeques, horse doovers consist of a packet of chips and some dip. But here are a few fancier ideas.

Fair Dinkum Cheese Balls

Makes 40 horse doovers

You will need a grater and large mixing bowl

Ingredients

250 g tasty cheddar cheese, grated
250 g Aussie Edam cheese, grated
250 g cream cheese
1/2 cup diced ham
1/2 cup diced red capsicum
1/4 cup diced spring onion
1/4 cup diced gherkin

Method

Mix the cheeses in a large bowl, until well combined. Mix in the remaining ingredients. Roll teaspoonfuls of the mixture into little balls. Chill before serving so that they firm up. Serve with crackers. Yum yum, pig's bum.

Swaggie in a Blanket

Makes 20 horse doovers

You will need toothpicks and an airtight container or cling wrap

Ingredients

20 slices white bread
250 g softened cream cheese
2 tins asparagus

Method

Spread a slice of bread with some cream cheese. Lay one asparagus spear diagonally across it. Wrap the bread around the asparagus and pin with a toothpick. Repeat until you have made all 20. Place in an airtight plastic container or cover with cling wrap and chill for at least 20 minutes before serving.

A swaggie is the nickname for a swagman. They were called swagmen because they carried a swag or bundle of belongings over their shoulder as they travelled through the bush.

Echidna Delight

Makes 24 horse doovers

You will need toothpicks

Echidna Delight for sir?
Lovely!

Ingredients

1 large orange
250 g cheddar cheese, cubed
8 gherkins, each cut into 3
2 long cabanossi sausages, each cut into 12 chunks
24 cocktail pickled onions (a mix of red, white and green)

Method

Slice off bottom of orange to create a flat end, and sit the orange on a serving plate. Thread a chunk of cheese onto a toothpick, followed by a chunk of gherkin, cabanossi, then pickled onion. Push the loaded-up toothpick into the orange. Repeat until you have created a colourful, echidna-like object. It is a perfect centrepiece for the horse-doovers table.

Whacko the Chook!

From flamin' galahs to cookin' chook, Australia loves its birds!

Thighs, breasts and eggs—chooks have it all and are loved by most, so we have a few chook recipes for you below. In the old days, when chooks were hard to come by, people had to rely on bush birds. Birds like bush turkeys, cockatoos, parrots and pigeons were all boiled, fried and stewed! We have included a classic Aussie bird recipe here for you to try (or not).

Scrambled Googs

Serves 1

You will need a mixing bowl and a saucepan

Ingredients

2 eggs
Salt and pepper
2 tablespoons milk (or cream)
1 teaspoon butter

In Australia, eggs can also be called googy eggs and cackleberries.

Method

Break the eggs into a bowl. Season with a pinch of salt and pepper. Add the milk (or cream). Beat with a fork until the whites and yolks are well mixed.

Melt the butter in a saucepan. Add the egg mixture and stir constantly over low heat. The mixture will begin to turn a pale yellowy-white. While the eggs are still soft and a little gooey, remove from heat. They will keep cooking in the hot pan even after you have taken it off the stove. Serve on hot buttered toast.

20

Cockatoo is off the menu!

Stewed Cockatoo

Serves 4, but you might still be hungry after

You will need a billy can

Ingredients

1 cockatoo (preferably not your neighbour's pet), plucked
Water
6 or so pebbles from a creek
Salt

Method

Place your cockatoo in a billy can. Fill with water. Add the pebbles and a pinch of salt. Boil for 2 or 3 days, adding water as necessary. When the pebbles are soft, chuck out the cockatoo and eat the pebbles.

Chook Nuggets

Serves 2

You will need a mixing bowl and large baking tray

Ingredients

250 g boneless skinless chicken breast
1 cup cornflakes
Salt
1/2 cup evaporated milk
Canola oil spray
Tomato or barbeque sauce

Method

Preheat the oven to 190°C. Grease a baking tray.

Cut the chicken into finger-sized lengths. Crush the cornflakes into fine crumbs and add a pinch of salt to the mix. Dip the chicken in the evaporated milk and then roll in the cornflake mixture. Place the chicken pieces on the baking tray, spray with canola oil and bake for 10 minutes or until golden brown. Serve with a bowl of tomato or barbeque sauce.

The Great Aussie Icon: Dinki-di Meat Pie

Ever heard a meat pie called a 'dog's eye'? Don't worry, pies don't really contain dogs' eyes. When you use a funny phrase that rhymes with something's real name, it's called rhyming slang.

You could say that the meat pie is one of Australia's favourite foods. Aussies eat around 500 million meat pies a year! It's the number-one food eaten at footy games. On AFL Grand Final Day at the MCG, over 90 000 pies are eaten. You would need a lot of tomato sauce for all those pies. It's estimated that around 500 000 tonnes of tomato sauce are used on meat pies in Australia each year.

Pie Floater

Serves 4

Ingredients

4 individual ready-made frozen meat pies
1 can ready-made pea soup
Tomato sauce (not really optional)

Method

Cook your pie and warm up your soup according to the instructions on the packaging. Ladle the soup into four separate bowls. Place a pie into each bowl of soup. Serve with tomato sauce.

22

Aussie Meat Pie

Serves 6

You will need a large bowl, a large frying pan, a 25 cm pie dish, baking paper, pie weights (or dried lentils or beans will do) and a pastry brush

Ingredients

700 g lean beef steak, cut into 2 cm cubes

2 tablespoons plain flour

1/4 cup vegetable oil

1 brown onion, chopped

1 1/4 cups beef stock

Salt and pepper

1 sheet ready-made shortcrust pastry

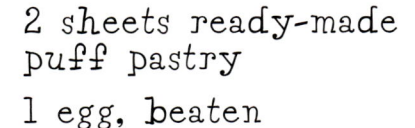

2 sheets ready-made puff pastry

1 egg, beaten

Tomato sauce

Method

Place the beef in a bowl and coat with the flour. Heat 2 tablespoons of the oil in a frying pan and cook the beef over medium heat until lightly browned on all sides. You might have to do this in batches, adding a little extra oil if necessary. Transfer to a bowl.

Reduce the heat slightly and add the remaining oil. Add the onion and cook for 2 minutes. Return the beef to the pan, along with the stock and a little salt and pepper. Simmer, covered, over low heat for 1 hour or until the meat is tender.

Increase the heat and cook uncovered for 10 minutes until the sauce thickens. Remove from the heat and allow to cool. Chill in the fridge for 30 minutes.

While the meat mixture is cooling, preheat the oven to 180°C and grease the pie dish. Lay the shortcrust pastry in the pie dish. Cut off any excess pastry that hangs over the sides, cover with baking paper and spread the pie weights on top. Bake for 15 minutes. (This is called blind-baking—where you cook the pastry before the filling is added.) Remove from the oven and spoon in the cooled beef filling. Increase the oven temperature to 200°C. Cover the pie with the puff pastry sheets and trim off any overhang. Brush the top with the egg and bake for 25 minutes. Remove and enjoy with plenty of tomato sauce.

Grandpa Bruce's Great Aussie BBQ

The Aussie barbeque is the natural habitat for many Aussies, especially during our long, hot summers. Generally, the sheilas make salads in the kitchen, the blokes guard the barbeque, the kids run amok in the backyard, and everyone swats flies.

On the next few pages you will find some bonza barbeque recipes, including steak, burgers, sausages and prawns!

Throw another snag, prawn or whatever-you-like on the barbie!

Grandpa Bruce, BBQ king.

GRANDMA BRUCE

Auntie Bev

Cousin Cassie

Jimbo's Jumbo Steaks

Serves 4

You will need a barbeque

Ingredients

4 large topside steaks

Tomato sauce

Method

Fire up the barbie till it's hot, hot, hot. Place the steak on the barbie. Cook for 5 minutes. Turn steak over. Cook for a further 5 minutes. The golden rule of barbequed steak: turn it only once. Serve on a plate with tomato sauce and maybe some salad.

Prawn Skewers

Serves 4

You will need a barbeque and skewers

Ingredients

12 green king prawns, shelled and deveined

2 cloves garlic, crushed

2 tablespoons honey

2 tablespoons soy sauce

1 tablespoon lemon juice

Method

Combine all the ingredients in a large bowl, cover and leave in the fridge for at least 30 minutes (preferably for a few hours).

Thread the prawns onto the skewers, and whack them on a hot barbeque. Cook for 2–3 minutes on each side.

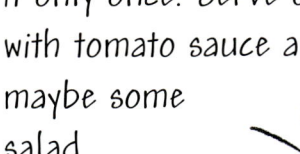

It's a Rissole, Love!

There is nothing better than a few rissoles from the barbie.

Hi... I'm Auntie Bev and you'll love my rissoles, or else.

Auntie Bev's Rissoles

Makes about 12 rissoles

You will need a large bowl, cling wrap and a barbeque

Ingredients

500 g beef mince
1 onion, grated
3/4 cup fresh breadcrumbs
2 tablespoons plain flour
1 egg
Salt and pepper
1 tablespoon tomato sauce
2 tablespoons fresh parsley, chopped
1 egg, extra, beaten
2 cups dried breadcrumbs
2 tablespoons oil

Method

Mix all of the ingredients in a bowl, except for the beaten egg, dried breadcrumbs and oil. Mould the mixture into small hand-sized patties. Dip the patties into the beaten egg and roll them in the dried breadcrumbs. Place on a plate, cover with cling wrap and chill them in the fridge for 30 minutes.

Fire up the barbie, add the oil to the hotplate and cook the patties for 3 minutes on each side or until they turn a dark brown. You can test to see whether they are cooked by cutting one patty in half. If it is still pink, turn the heat down and cook through.

Uncle Daz's Mega BBQ Burger

Makes 6 burgers

You will need a barbeque

Ingredients

Mayonnaise

Tomato sauce

6 white rolls, cut in half

6 rissoles, cooked on the barbie (see Auntie Bev's Rissoles recipe)

2 onions, sliced and fried on the barbie

6 slices tasty cheddar cheese

6 rashers bacon, cooked on the barbie

6 leaves iceberg lettuce, shredded

3 tomatoes, thinly sliced

6 slices canned beetroot

6 rings tinned pineapple

6 eggs, fried on the barbie

Uncle Daz, working his mince magic.

Uncle Daz, lovingly tenderising his mince.

Method

Spread a little of the mayonnaise and tomato sauce on the base of each roll. Top with a rissole, more tomato sauce, some onion, a slice of cheese, a rasher of bacon, some lettuce, slices of tomato, beetroot, pineapple and a fried egg. Cover with the top half of the roll. Try to wrap your laughing gear around that.

Bangers, Snags and Mystery Bags

Your Gramps or Gran might remember the days when a sausage was called a saveloy. Ask them if they've ever heard the phrase, 'Fair suck of the sav'. During the Great Depression, families used to share just one sausage between them for dinner. They'd pull it out of the stew and each have a tasty suck. If someone took too long, Little Johnny, waiting patiently for his turn, would yell out, 'Hey! Fair suck of the sav! It's my turn!' That's where some people think this saying came from.

Fair suck of the sav!

Throw a snag on the barbie—the question is, what sort?

- saveloy or sav
- lamb snag
- chook snag
- beef snag
- tofu snag
- pork snag
- kanga banger
- mystery bag

What's in a Name?

Beef Snag
Cow sausage

Pork Snag
Pig sausage

Chook Snag
Chicken sausage

Lamb Snag
Sheep sausage

Tofu Snag
The vegetarian alternative, only just becoming acceptable at Aussie barbeques. These sausages cause less offence than they used to.

Kanga Banger
Skippy sausage, otherwise known as kangaroo sausage. In many ways, this is a true-blue Aussie sausage.

Sav or Saveloy
The old-school term for sausage. Usually it meant what we would call a frankfurt.

Frankfurt
A reddish, rubbery Mystery Bag of a sausage that definitely doesn't belong on the barbeque. They are boiled or steamed and used in hotdogs.

Mystery Bag
Who knows what kind of meat?

Snags on the Barbie

Makes 8 snags

You will need a barbeque

Ingredients
8 snags, any type (except frankfurt)

Vegetable or olive oil, enough to thinly cover the barbeque plate

Method
Turn on the barbeque to a medium heat. Coat the hotplate with a thin layer of oil. Lightly prick the snags with a fork. Place them on the barbeque and cook for about 20 minutes, turning every 5 minutes so that the snags cook evenly. Serve with tomato sauce in a roll or with salad.

Fish 'n' Chips Down Under

Did you know that in Australia people eat sharks much more often than sharks eat people? Next time you are at your fish 'n' chip shop, ask for a great white with chips. If the shopkeeper looks at you strangely, ask for flake instead. Flake is any species of small shark, and is commonly used in your regular battered fish 'n' chip takeaway.

Cooking your own Aussie fish 'n' chips isn't hard if you know how.

What'll it be?

I'm just deciding.

Despite what your dad might say, spuds (otherwise known as potatoes) grow in the ground, not behind your ears. So the first thing you have to do is give your spuds a good wash to get the soil off. If you were a swaggie, you would then take out your knife—the one you use for shaving, hunting and trimming your toenails—and you'd use it to slice away the spud skin. But, because you're probably not a swaggie, grab a potato peeler from the kitchen drawer. Carefully peel all the skin off. Then give the spuds another wash.

Chunky Chips

Serves 4–6

You will need 1 or 2 deep oven trays (or roasting tins), tongs and paper towel

Ingredients

6 spuds, peeled and washed
2 cups vegetable oil
Salt
White vinegar

Method

Preheat the oven to 180°C. Cut the potatoes into slices 2 cm wide. Cut each slice into long sticks, each about 2 cm wide.

Pour oil into a deep oven tray, to a depth of about 1 cm. Place your spud sticks in a single layer in the oil. Bake for 30 minutes. Turn the chips over and return to the oven for another 30 minutes. Remove from the oven, place on paper towel to drain off the oil and sprinkle with a little salt and a splash of vinegar.

You-Beaut Snapper

Serves 4

You will need a mixing bowl, deep frying pan or large saucepan, eggflip and paper towel

Ingredients

4 snapper fillets
3/4 cup plain flour
Salt and pepper
1 egg, beaten
3/4 cup water
Vegetable oil

Method

Pat the fish fillets dry with a paper towel.

Mix the flour and a little salt and pepper in a bowl. Make a well in the centre of the flour, add the beaten egg and mix well. Add the water slowly, stirring all the time. Stir the batter until smooth.

Pour oil into a frying pan, to a depth of about 4 cm. Heat the oil over high heat. Meanwhile, dip each fillet in the batter for a few seconds and allow any excess batter to drip off.

Once oil is hot, place fillets in the pan. Deep-fry for 5 minutes, turn the fillets over using an eggflip, then fry for another 5 minutes or until cooked through. Drain on paper towel. Serve with Chunky Chips.

Bush Tucker

Indigenous Australians have gathered, cooked and eaten bush tucker for more than 50 000 years. Australia is a very large continent and each of the different regions has slightly different bush tucker. Some of the wild foods you can find around Australia include all sorts of fish, crabs, prawns, octopus, lizards, kangaroos, emus and their eggs, turtles, berries, nuts, yams and lilly pillies. And there are many traditional ways of cooking these foods—smoking, barbequing and stewing, to name but a few.

When the white fellas turned up in Australia, they didn't have this knowledge. They didn't have a clue what to eat and some of them starved even though they were surrounded by plenty of excellent bush tucker. They could have had food like sugarbag honey, wattle seeds, barbequed emu, crocodile curry, kangaroo stew, smoked barramundi wrapped in native ginger leaves and sun-dried bush tomatoes.

Here's a fair-dinkum Aussie recipe using traditional Australian ingredients, as well as a few introduced ones.

Some feral bush tucker on the boil

Roo Stew with Bush Tomatoes

Serves 4

You will need a deep frying pan or large saucepan

You can find dried bush tomatoes in some gourmet food stores. Bush tomatoes grow in the very arid desert areas of Central Australia.

Ingredients

2 tablespoons olive oil
500 g kangaroo fillet, cubed
1 onion, diced
1 cup beef stock
1 carrot, diced
1 stick celery, diced
4 bush tomatoes (or any tomatoes will do), diced
1–2 teaspoons cornflour
1/2 cup water

Method

Heat the oil in frying pan or saucepan. Add the kangaroo meat and onion, and fry for 5 minutes or until just browned. Add the stock, reduce the heat and simmer for 25 minutes. Add the carrot, celery and tomatoes, and simmer for a further 25 minutes. To thicken the sauce, stir the cornflour into 1/2 cup cold water and add this to the stew. Simmer for a further 5 minutes before serving.

Some bush tucker may need coaxing into your pot.

From Over Yonder to Down Under

Since the time when only the Indigenous Australians lived here, many people from different cultures have arrived on this continent, and they have brought with them all sorts of delicious grub. The Chinese do some top stuff with pork; the Greeks with yoghurts, olives and cheese; and the Lebanese with hoummos, tabouli and chook kebabs. Australia is truly a lucky country to have so many different cooks who know how to make good food.

Here are two modern Aussie favourites.

Did you know that spag bol is Australia's favourite meal of all time?

Spag Bol from Italy to Ingham

Serves 4–6

You will need a frying pan and large saucepan

Ingredients

2 tablespoons olive oil
1 onion, diced
1 clove garlic, crushed
500 g beef mince
1 cup beef stock
400 g tin chopped tomatoes
2 tablespoons tomato paste
Salt and pepper
Handful fresh basil leaves, roughly chopped
500 g dried spaghetti
1 cup grated parmesan

Method

Heat the oil in a frying pan over medium heat and fry the onion and garlic until softened. Add the mince and stir until browned. Add the stock, tomatoes, tomato paste, a pinch of salt and pepper, and simmer for 15 minutes. Stir through the basil.

Meanwhile, cook the spaghetti according to the packet instructions. Serve the spaghetti with mince sauce on top and a sprinkle of parmesan.

Nachos from Mexico to Mandurah

Serves 4

You will need a baking tray and a blender

Ingredients

2 x 400 g tins red kidney beans
400 g tin crushed tomatoes
3 cloves garlic, crushed
1 large packet cheese-flavoured corn chips
250 g cheddar cheese, grated
Sour cream
1 avocado, mashed
Tomato salsa

Method

Preheat the oven to 180°C. Place the beans, tomato and garlic in a blender, and blend until mixed but a little chunky. Spread the corn chips on a baking tray. Pour the bean mixture over the chips. Sprinkle the cheese over the top and bake for 30 minutes. Remove from the oven and place in serving bowls. Serve with a dollop each of sour cream, avocado and salsa.

Dessert Dames

Perhaps it's the big frilly skirts or the big bouffants of our buxom dames that always seem to inspire a dessert.

Dame Nellie Melba was Australia's first internationally acclaimed opera singer way back in the 1890s. When she performed at the Royal Opera House, in Covent Garden, London, she was treated to a big fancy dinner. Some people liked to serve custard tarts to opera singers, but legendary French chef, Auguste Escoffier, enraptured by Nellie, served her peaches and cream in a large swan shaped out of ice. It caused quite a stir, and the dessert has been a hit ever since.

A more recent Dame of Australia, Edna, known for her love of possums and gladioli, now has her very own dessert. The Edna Split is named in her honour by yours truly, Ruthie May.

Peach Melba

Serves 6

You will need a large saucepan, a blender and sieve

Ingredients

750 ml water

250 g caster sugar

6 peaches, halved and stones removed

375 g raspberries (fresh or frozen)

100 g icing sugar

Vanilla ice-cream

Method

Place the water and sugar in a large saucepan and heat until the sugar has dissolved and the mixture becomes syrupy. Bring to the boil. Carefully drop the peaches into the syrup and allow to simmer for 3–5 minutes. When the peaches are soft, remove from the pan and place on a plate. Peel off the peach skins and discard, and allow the peaches to cool.

To make the sauce, blend the raspberries and icing sugar until smooth. Push the sauce through a sieve to make it even smoother.

To assemble, place two scoops of ice-cream and two peach halves in each bowl. Pour the raspberry sauce on top.

Edna Split

Serves 1

You will need a mixing bowl

Ingredients

2 scoops vanilla ice-cream

Blue food colouring

Red food colouring

1 banana

Chocolate topping

Crushed nuts

Method

Scoop the ice-cream into a mixing bowl. Add one drop each of blue and red food colouring and mix well. The ice-cream will turn purple. Return to the freezer for at least 15 minutes.

Split the banana in half lengthways and arrange in a dessert bowl. Take the ice-cream out of the freezer and scoop on top of the banana pieces. Cover in chocolate topping and sprinkle with crushed nuts.

37

All Over, Pavlova

It's a bit of an Aussie tradition to shorten the name of nearly everything. Instead of Pamela we have Pam and instead of Pavlova we have Pav.

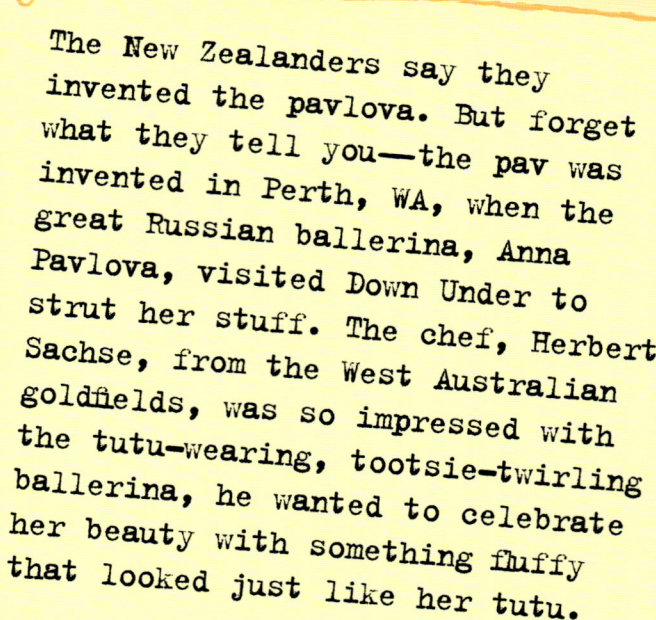

The New Zealanders say they invented the **pavlova**. But forget what they tell you—the **pav** was invented in Perth, WA, when the great Russian ballerina, Anna Pavlova, visited Down Under to strut her stuff. The chef, Herbert Sachse, from the West Australian goldfields, was so impressed with the tutu-wearing, tootsie-twirling ballerina, he wanted to celebrate her beauty with something fluffy that looked just like her tutu.

Pam's Pav

Serves 6–8

You will need a large baking tray, baking paper, an electric mixer and a spatula

Ingredients

6 egg whites
Salt
1 1/2 cups caster sugar
1 teaspoon white vinegar
1/2 teaspoon vanilla essence
300 ml cream, whipped
1 cup sliced strawberries

The placement of the strawberries

Pam whisks while hungry neighbours pry.

Method

Preheat the oven to 200°C. Lightly grease a baking tray and line it with baking paper.

Using an electric mixer, beat the egg whites with a pinch of salt until stiff peaks form. Continue beating, gradually adding the sugar. Add the vinegar and vanilla. Beat until the mixture feels heavy and stiff peaks form.

Spoon the mixture onto the baking tray and use a spatula to form a big round circle. Reduce the heat of the oven to 150°C and bake for 1½ hours. Don't open the oven door to peek at your pav. If you do, the hot air will escape and your pav will go flat. Remove the pav from oven when it is golden brown on top, and allow to cool on its baking tray. Once cool, decorate with the cream and strawberries.

Index

A

adult supervision 4
Anzac Biscuits 12, 13
Anzac Day 12
Auntie Bev's Rissoles 26
Aussie Chrissie Damper 9
Aussie Meat Pie 23

B

Banana benders (banana skewers) 17
barbeque foods
    Jimbo's Jumbo Steaks 25
    Prawn Skewers 25
    Snags on the Barbie 29
    Uncle Daz's Mega BBQ Burger 27
Berry Shake 7
Beryl's Bonza Scones 14
Billabong Surprise 17
Billy Loaf 9
Billy Tea 6, 7
biscuits 12–13
    Anzac Biscuits 12, 13
bread
    Bush-Pig Fairy Bread 10
    damper 8, 9
        Aussie Chrissie 9
        Billy Loaf 9
        with Cocky's Joy 9
    Swaggie in a Blanket 19
burger 27
Bush-Pig Fairy Bread 10
bush tucker 32–33
    Roo Stew with Bush Tomatoes 33

C

chicken 20–21
    Chook Nuggets 21
chips 30–31
chocolate
    Banana Benders 17
    Roo Doo in a Patty Case (chocolate crackles) 15
Chook Nuggets 21
Chunky Chips 31
Cocky's Joy (golden syrup) 9, 13
cook's tools 5

D

damper *see* bread
Damper with Cocky's Joy 9
desserts
    Banana Benders 17
    Billabong Surprise 17
    Dinky-di Icy Poles 17
    Edna Split 37
    Frogs in the Billabong 16
    Joe Blakes in the Billabong 17
    Pam's Pav 39
    Peach Melba 37
Dinky-di Icy Poles 17
drinks 6–7
    Berry Shake 7
    Billy Tea 6, 7
    Redback Spider 7

E

Echidna Delight 19
Edna Split 37
eggs
    Scrambled Googs 20
Esky 16–17

F

Fair Dinkum Cheese Balls 18
fish
    You-Beaut Snapper 31
fish and chips 30–31
Frogs in the Billabong 16
fruit
    Aussie Chrissie Damper 9
    Banana Benders 17
    Berry Shake 7
    Echidna Delight 19
    Edna Split 37
    Pam's Pav 39
    Peach Melba 37

G

golden syrup *see* Cocky's Joy
Great Depression 28

H

Horse doovers (*hors d'oeuvres*) 18–19
    Echidna Delight 19
    Fair Dinkum Cheese Balls 18
    Swaggie in a Blanket 19

I

icy poles 17
Indigenous Australians 8, 32, 34

J

jelly 16, 17
    Billabong Surprise 17
    Frogs in the Billabong 16
    Joe Blakes in the Billabong 17
Jimbo's Jumbo Steaks 25
Joe Blakes in the Billabong 17

L

Lamington, Lord 11
lamingtons 10, 11
Lord Lamington's Lamingtons 11

M

meat pies 22–23
Melba, Dame Nellie 36

N

Nachos from Mexico to Mandurah 35

O

Oldie 4, 5

P

Pam's Pav 39
pavlova 38, 39
Pavlova, Anna 38
Peach Melba 37
Pie Floater 22
Pikelets 11
potatoes *see* spuds
Prawn Skewers 25
pumpkin scones 15

Q

Queensland Blue Pumpkin Scones 15

R

Redback Spider (drink) 7
rissoles 26
Roo Doo in a Patty Case (chocolate crackles) 15
Roo Stew with Bush Tomatoes 33

S

sausages 28–29
    various kinds of 29
scones
    Beryl's Bonza Scones 14
    Queensland Blue Pumpkin Scones 15
Scrambled Googs (scrambled eggs) 20
slang
    Australian, usage in *Stew a Cockatoo* 2
    rhyming 17, 22
Snags on the Barbie 29
soup
    Pie Floater 22
Spag Bol from Italy to Ingham (spaghetti bolognese) 35
spuds
    Chunky Chips 31
    how to peel 30
steaks 25
Stewed Cockatoo 21
Swaggie in a Blanket 19
swagmen 19, 30

T

tea
    billy 6, 7

U

Uncle Daz's Mega BBQ Burger 27
utensils *see* cook's tools

W

World War I 12

Y

You-Beaut Snapper 31